AF251612

Jumpstarters for the Human Body

Short Daily Warm-ups for the Classroom

By
WENDI SILVANO

COPYRIGHT © 2007 Mark Twain Media, Inc.

ISBN 978-1-58037-430-9

Printing No. CD-404079

Mark Twain Media, Inc., Publishers
Distributed by Carson-Dellosa Publishing LLC

Visit us at www.carsondellosa.com

The purchase of this book entitles the buyer to reproduce the student pages for classroom use only. Other permissions may be obtained by writing Mark Twain Media, Inc., Publishers.

All rights reserved. Printed in the United States of America.

Table of Contents

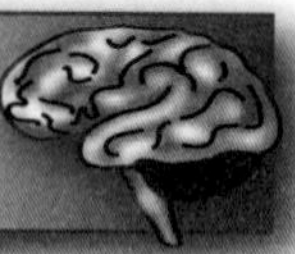

 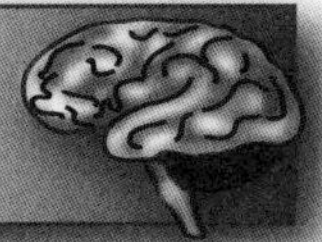

Introduction to the Teacher

It is important for students to periodically review the information they have previously learned. Jumpstarters help students do just that while also preparing them for the day's lesson by focusing on the topic of study.

The short warm-up activities in this book provide activities that help students review what they have learned. Each page contains five warm-ups (one for each day of the school week).

Suggestions for using warm-up activities:

- Copy and cut apart one page each week. Give students one warm-up activity each day at the beginning of class.

- Give each student a copy of the entire page to keep in their binders to complete as assigned.

- Make transparencies of individual warms-ups and complete activities as a group.

- Put copies of warm-ups in a learning center for students to complete on their own when they have a few extra minutes.

- Use warm-ups as homework assignments.

- Use warm-ups as questions in a review game.

- Keep some warm-ups on hand to use when the class has a few extra minutes before dismissal.

Human Body Warm-ups: Body Organization

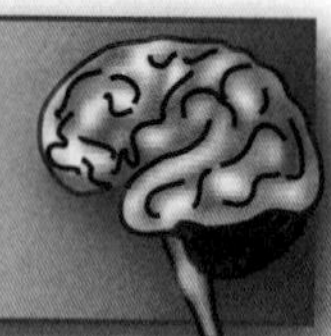

Name/Date __________________________

Body Organization 1

Match each of these cell parts with their jobs.

_C_ 1. nucleus

_D_ 2. nuclear membrane

_B_ 3. cytoplasm

_A_ 4. cell membrane

a. jelly-like material around the outside of the nucleus

b. controls movement of material in and out of the cell

c. controls the activities of the cell

d. surrounds the nucleus to keep the parts inside

Name/Date __________________________

Body Organization 2

Label this diagram of a cell. Use the terms listed below.

nucleus   **vacuole**   **cytoplasm**
nuclear membrane   **cell membrane**

neclevs   _vaevole_

nuclear mem   _cytoplasm_

cell mem.

Name/Date __________________________

Body Organization 3

Tell if each is a tissue, organ, or system. Write "T," "O," or "S."

1. heart _O_   2. respiratory _S_
3. bone _T_   4. skeletal _S_
5. muscle _T_   6. kidney _O_
7. brain _O_   8. nerve _T_
9. digestive _S_   10. pancreas _O_

Name/Date __________________________

Body Organization 4

Which body system…

1. Carries blood throughout the body?
   cardiovascular
2. Disposes of waste material?
   digestive
3. Gives structure and form to the body?
   skeletal
4. Provides the body with oxygen?
   respiratory

Name/Date __________________________

Body Organization 5

Which body system…

1. Moves the body parts? _muscular_
2. Sends signals to control all the other systems? _nervous_
3. Uses chemicals (hormones) to help control other systems? _endocrine_
4. Breaks down foods to nourish the body?
   digestive

Human Body Warm-ups:
Skeletal System

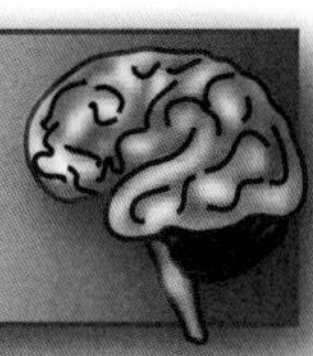

Name/Date ___________________________

Skeletal System 1

List three organs that are protected by the skeletal system.

1. ___________________________
2. ___________________________
3. ___________________________

Name/Date ___________________________

Skeletal System 2

Fill in the blanks.

1. Red bone ___________________ is where red and white blood cells are made.
2. ___________________ cells are stored in yellow bone marrow.
3. The skeletal system works with the ___________________ system to move the parts of the body.

Name/Date ___________________________

Skeletal System 3

Unscramble these four parts of the skeletal system.

1. snebo ___________________
2. glaectira ___________________
3. mgstliaen ___________________
4. itsnoj ___________________

Name/Date ___________________________

Skeletal System 4

1. How is the skeletal system like a factory? ___________
____
____

2. How is the skeletal system like a storehouse? ___________
____
____

Name/Date ___________________________
____

Skeletal System 5

Write "Yes" or "No" to indicate if each of these is a job of the skeletal system.

______ 1. shapes and supports the body

______ 2. transmits messages to all parts of the body

______ 3. protects organs

______ 4. works with the muscular system to move parts of the body

______ 5. helps rid the body of wastes

______ 6. warehouses fat cells, calcium, and other minerals

Human Body Warm-ups: Skeletal System

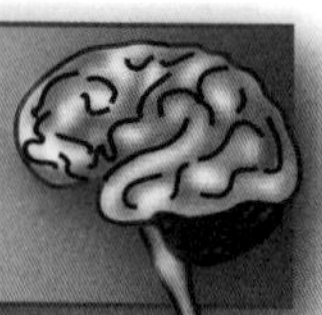

Name/Date __________________

____

Skeletal System 16

Identify the type of fracture described below.

greenstick fracture

simple fracture

compound fracture

1. Which type of fracture is when the bone is completely broken and the skin is broken too?

   ____

2. Which type of fracture is a break in the bone that does not go all the way through the bone?

   ____

3. Which type of fracture is where the bone has broken all the way through, but the skin is not broken?

   ____

Name/Date __________________

Skeletal System 17

1. Why is it so important to have a proper diet during your growing years? __________________ __________________

2. What is ossification? __________________ __________________

Name/Date __________________

Skeletal System 18

Number these four steps of ossification in the order they happen.

_______ a. calcium compounds stay in the cells

_______ b. bone cells absorb calcium

_______ c. calcium is changed to calcium compounds

_______ d. calcium compounds harden and become bone

Name/Date __________________

Skeletal System 19

Calculate the approximate weight of your bones using this formula:

Your weight times 35 divided by 100

____

Name/Date __________________

Skeletal System 20

Write "T" for true or "F" for false.

_______ 1. Bones have blood vessels and nerves in them.

_______ 2. Babies' skeletal systems are mostly cartilage.

_______ 3. Calcium is an important mineral for bone strength.

_______ 4. The center of the bone is the hardest part.

 # Human Body Warm-ups: Skeletal System 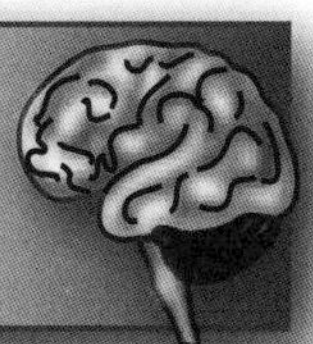

Name/Date _______________________

Skeletal System 21

Fill in the missing vowels of these regions of the spinal column

1. c __ r v __ c __ l
2. c __ c c y g __ __ l
3. t h __ r __ c __ c
4. l __ m b __ r
5. s __ c r __ l

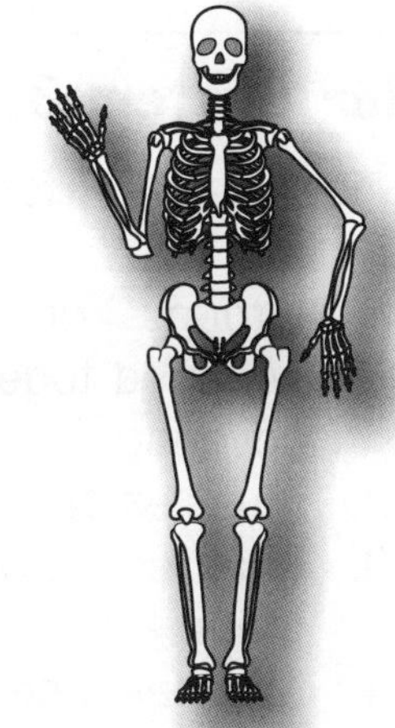

Name/Date _______________________

Skeletal System 22

Circle the bone that is connected to the one listed.

1. femur:		scapula		patella
2. ulna:		radius		clavicle
3. tibia:		fibula		coccyx
4. rib:		phalanges		sternum

Name/Date _______________________

Skeletal System 23

Write "T" for true or "F" for false.

_____ 1. The humerus is below the ulna.

_____ 2. The tibia is connected to the patella.

_____ 3. The coccyx is at the very bottom of the spinal column.

_____ 4. The clavicle is part of the leg.

_____ 5. The mandible is below the sternum.

Name/Date _______________________

Skeletal System 24

Label these bones in the skeletal system on the diagram on page 36.

cranium	ribs	femur
vertebrae	pelvis	mandible
humerus	patella	phalanges
metatarsals		

Name/Date _______________________

Skeletal System 25

Number these bones in order from the top (#1) of the body to the bottom (#8).

_____ femur			_____ cranium

_____ ribs			_____ radius

_____ carpals			_____ clavicle

_____ metatarsals			_____ tibia

 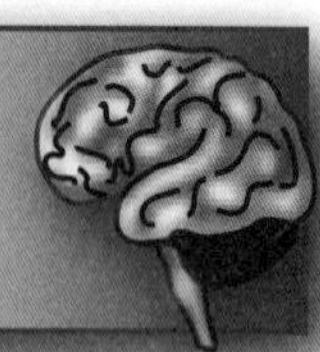

Human Body Warm-ups: Muscular System

Name/Date __________________________

Muscular System 1

1. __________________________ and __________________________ are the two kinds of protein in a muscle cell.

2. They __________________ past each other, and that makes a muscle cell work.

Name/Date __________________________

Muscular System 2

Males are about 40% muscle, and females are about 35% muscle.

1. If a boy weighs 110 pounds, about how much of his weight is from muscles? _______________

2. If a girl weighs 80 pounds, about how much of her weight is from muscles? _________

Name/Date __________________________

Muscular System 3

Write "T" for true or "F" for false.

______ 1. Groups of muscle fibers are wrapped together inside a special covering.

______ 2. Muscles are not living tissue.

______ 3. Muscles have nerve tissue in them.

______ 4. Muscles need oxygen and nutrients.

Name/Date __________________________

Muscular System 4

Unscramble the three main parts of the muscular system.

1. ucsmels __________________

2. stneond __________________

3. lmsitgnae __________________

Name/Date __________________________

Muscular System 5

Circle the correct answer.

1. There are more than ______ muscles in your body   650   200

2. Groups of muscle tissue are organs.   True   False

3. ______ is the basic unit of a muscle.   protein   muscle cell

 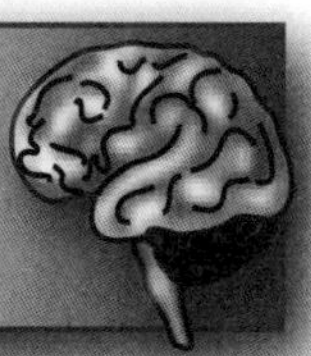

Human Body Warm-ups: Muscular System

Name/Date ______________________________

Muscular System 6

Explain the difference between a voluntary muscle and an involuntary muscle. Give an example of each kind.

____

____

____

____

Name/Date ______________________________

Muscular System 7

Draw lines to match these three types of muscles to their scientific names.

1. skeletal muscles   a. visceral muscles

2. smooth muscles   b. cardiac muscles

3. heart muscles   c. striated muscles

Name/Date ______________________________

Muscular System 8

Write "V" for voluntary muscles or "I" for involuntary muscles.

_____ 1. heart muscles   _____ 2. jaw muscles

_____ 3. leg muscles   _____ 4. arm muscles

_____ 5. finger muscles   _____ 6. small intestine muscles

_____ 7. blood vessel muscles   _____ 8. foot muscles

Can you name one muscle that can be both? ______________________________

Name/Date ______________________________

Muscular System 9

Write "S" for skeletal, or striated, muscle; "V" for visceral, or smooth, muscle; or "C" for cardiac muscle.

_____ 1. heart muscle

_____ 2. arm muscle

_____ 3. muscles that line the digestive tract

_____ 4. leg muscle

_____ 5. muscles that line the blood vessels

Name/Date ______________________________

Muscular System 10

Write "T" for true or "F" for false.

_____ 1. When a muscle contracts, it gets longer.

_____ 2. After a muscle contracts, it relaxes.

_____ 3. Most muscles work in pairs.

_____ 4. Smooth muscles can stay contracted for long periods of time.

 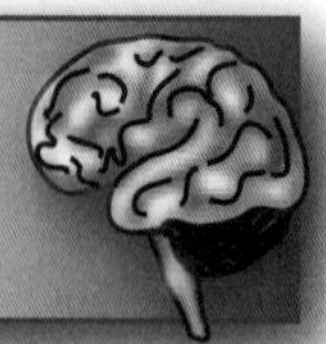

Human Body Warm-ups: Muscular System

Name/Date ____

Muscular System 11

Fill in the blanks with these words: **contract, overstretched, oxygen, exercise, strain, cramp**

1. If you don't warm up before you exercise, your muscle might ________________________ involuntarily, causing a ________________________.
2. When you ________________________, or work your muscles, they need extra food and ________________________.
3. If a muscle gets ________________________, it causes an injury called a ________________________.

Name/Date ________________________________

Muscular System 12

Number these steps in order to explain how your arm moves.

______ a. The biceps contracts, which raises the arm, and the triceps relaxes.
______ b. The brain sends a message to move your arm.
______ c. The message travels through nerves connected to single muscle fibers.
______ d. The biceps relaxes, straightening the arm, and the triceps contracts.

Name/Date ________________________________

Muscular System 13

Write "Yes" or "No" to indicate if each of these is a type of movement controlled by smooth muscles.

______ 1. moving blood through blood vessels
______ 2. opening and closing eyelids
______ 3. pushing food through the digestive tract
______ 4. widening the pupils in the eyes

Name/Date ________________________________

Muscular System 14

What muscle am I? ________________________________

Clue one: I am the most important muscle involved in breathing.

Clue two: I am a sheet of thin, flat muscle.

Clue three: If I get irritated, I cause the hiccups.

Name/Date ________________________________

Muscular System 15

1. What does weight-lifting do for your muscles? ________________________________ ________________________________

2. How does aerobic exercise help the cardiac muscle? ________________________________ ________________________________ ________________________________

Human Body Warm-ups: Muscular System

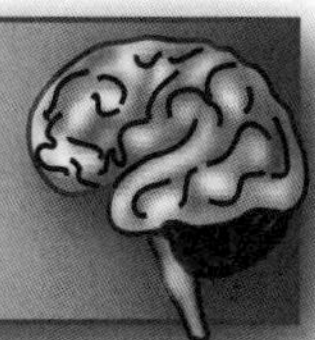

Name/Date _______________________

Muscular System 16

Write "T" for true or "F" for false.

______ 1. Your pulse is the feeling of your blood moving through your blood vessels.

______ 2. The average heart rate is around 150 beats per minute.

______ 3. The beating of your heart is a voluntary muscle movement.

______ 4. You can usually feel your pulse in your neck and wrist.

Name/Date _______________________

Muscular System 17

Fill in each blank with either the word *bone* or the word *muscle*.

1. Ligaments connect

_______________ to _______________.

2. Tendons attach _______________ to

_______________.

Name/Date _______________________

Muscular System 18

Fill in each blank with the correct muscle type.

1. A(n) _______________ muscle causes a joint to bend when it contracts.

2. A(n) _______________ muscle causes a joint to straighten when it contracts.

Name/Date _______________________

Muscular System 19

Place the correct letter on each blank.
a. tendonitis b. insertion c. sprain d. origin

1. ______ is the end of the muscle that does not move.

2. ______ is the end of the muscle that can move.

3. ______ is a swelling of the tendons.

4. A ______ is a ligament, muscle, or tendon that has been stretched too far.

Name/Date _______________________

Muscular System 20

Write each of these muscle names next to the area of the body where it is found.

pectoral   **masseter**   **soleus**   **deltoid**   **quadriceps**
intercostals   **triceps**   **gluteus maximus**   **tibialis**

Arm & Hand: _______________________________________

Leg & Foot: _______________________________________

Head & Trunk: _______________________________________

 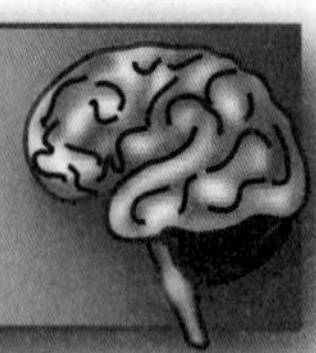

Human Body Warm-ups: Muscular System

Name/Date _______________________

Muscular System 21

Why is it important to your muscles that you eat healthily, exercise, and get enough sleep?

____

____

____

____

Name/Date _______________________

Muscular System 22

Your muscle will hurt if you work it too hard because it doesn't get enough o_____________.

This produces l____________ a__________,

which makes the muscle sore.

Name/Date _______________________

Muscular System 23

1. What is atrophy of the muscles?

____

____

2. What is hypertrophy of the muscles?

____

____

Name/Date _______________________

Muscular 24

Fill in the missing letters to identify each term.

1. Types of muscle that move bones

   s __ __ __ __ t __ __

2. A muscle that works automatically

   i __ __ __ __ __ n __ __ __ __

3. The type of muscle in the walls of the blood vessels   s __ __ __ __ __

Name/Date _______________________

Muscular System 25

Fill in the missing letters to identify each term.

1. These tissues attach bone to bone

   l __ __ __ m __ __ __ __ __

2. A muscle that can be controlled

   v __ __ __ __ __ __ __ __ __ y

3. These tissues connect bones to muscles

   t __ __ __ __ n __

 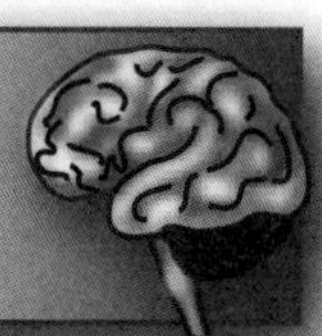

Human Body Warm-ups: Circulatory System

Name/Date _______________________

Circulatory System 1

On your own paper, rearrange the words in these mixed-up sentences to describe the two main jobs of the circulatory system.

1. oxygen the to cell every circulatory delivers in The food system and water body.

2. removes The cells system waste from circulatory the.

Name/Date _______________________

Circulatory System 2

Put check marks by those items that are jobs of the circulatory system.

_______ 1. maintaining body temperature
_______ 2. coordinating what you sense and feel
_______ 3. fighting diseases
_______ 4. carrying chemicals, food, water, and oxygen to cells

Name/Date _______________________

Circulatory System 3

Unscramble the names of these two main parts of the circulatory system and then tell what they do:

1. rtahe _______________________

2. doblo sevlses _______________________

Name/Date _______________________

Circulatory System 4

Write "T" for true or "F" for False.

_______ 1. The heart is one of the hardest working organs in your body.
_______ 2. The heart is about as big as your foot.
_______ 3. Your heart is in the middle of your chest.
_______ 4. The heart has three chambers.

Name/Date _______________________

____

Circulatory System 5

Circle all of the words in the list below that are part of the circulatory system.

platelets	intestines
aorta	plasma
kidney	heart
blood	artery
wrist	veins
nostril	valves
thyroid	oxygen
ventricle	bile
capillaries	skull

# Human Body Warm-ups:
Circulatory System
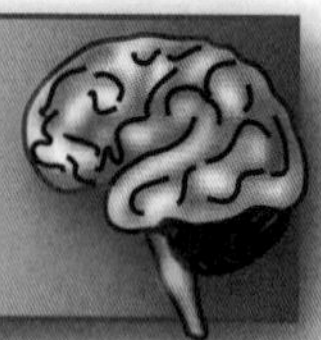

Name/Date _______________________

Circulatory System 6

Fill in the blanks with these words:
body, pumps, oxygen, cells, lungs

The heart is like two _____________ that work side by side. The right side pumps blood to the _____________ to get _____________. The left side of the heart pumps the oxygen-filled blood to everywhere else in the _____________ to take food, water, and oxygen to the _____________.

Name/Date _______________________

Circulatory System 7

Label these parts of the heart on the diagram on page 37.

right ventricle	**left ventricle**
pulmonary artery	**vena cava**
right atrium	**left atrium**
aorta septum	**pulmonary veins**

Name/Date _______________________

Circulatory System 8

Match each term with its definition.

_____ 1. Chambers that collect blood coming into the heart from the veins.

_____ 2. The body's largest artery—pumps blood out of the heart to most parts of the body

_____ 3. The main incoming blood vessels

_____ 4. Chambers that pump blood back to the body and lungs

a. aorta

b. vena cava

c. atriums

d. ventricles

Name/Date _______________________

Circulatory System 9

Number these tubes of the circulatory system in order from smallest to largest. Then tell what each does.

_____ a. veins _______________________

_____ b. capillaries _______________________

_____ c. arteries _______________________

Name/Date _______________________

Circulatory System 10

1. Why does your face get red when you are extra hot?

____

2. Why does skin look pale when you are extra cold?

____

Human Body Warm-ups:
Circulatory System

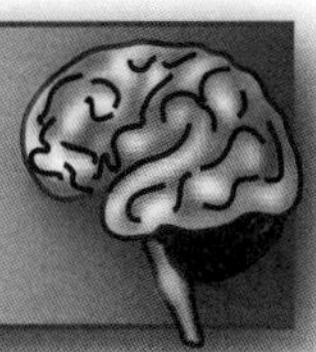

Name/Date _______________________________

Circulatory System 11

tricuspid valve   **pulmonary valve**   **mitral valve**   **aortic valve**

1. The _________________________ lets blood flow from the left ventricle, through the aorta, to most parts of the body.

2. The _________________________ lets blood flow from the right atrium into the right ventricle.

3. The _________________________ lets blood flow from the left atrium to the left ventricle.

4. The _________________________ lets blood flow from the right ventricle into the pulmonary artery.

Name/Date _______________________________

Circulatory System 12

Write "T" for true or "F" for false.

______ 1. The upper chambers of the heart are called ventricles.

______ 2. The lower chambers of the heart pump blood out of the heart.

______ 3. Blood can go both ways between the atria and the ventricles.

______ 4. Valves control the flow of blood from the atria to the ventricles.

Name/Date _______________________________

Circulatory System 13

What are valves, and why are they important to the circulatory system?

____

____

____

____

Name/Date _______________________________

Circulatory System 14

What am I? _______________________________

Clue one: I am a thick wall of muscle in the heart.

Clue two: I keep blood from the two sides of the heart from mixing.

Clue three: I am in between the right and left ventricle.

Name/Date _______________________________

Circulatory System 15

How does the circulatory system help medicines work when you are sick?

____

____

____

____

 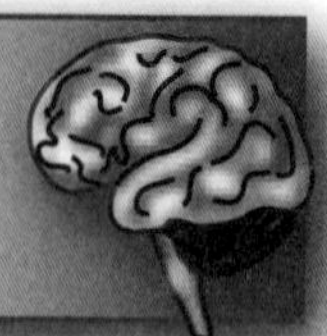

Human Body Warm-ups: Circulatory System

Name/Date _______________________________

Circulatory System 16

What are the four basic parts of blood?

1. p_______________________________
2. r_______________________________
3. w_______________________________
4. p_______________________________

Name/Date _______________________________

Circulatory System 17

Circle the facts about plasma that are correct.

1. Water makes up 90 percent of plasma.
2. Plasma has salts and other chemicals in it.
3. Plasma has no red or white blood cells in it.
4. Plasma carries wastes from the cells to where they will be removed.

Name/Date _______________________________

Circulatory System 18

carbon dioxide	**bone marrow**	**oxygen**
hemoglobin	**nucleus**	**lungs**

Red blood cells carry _______________ to all the cells in the body, and then pick up a waste called _______________ to carry to the _______________ where it is removed from the body. Red blood cells are made in the _______________. They are living cells, but they do not have a _______________.

Name/Date _______________________________

Circulatory System 19

What am I? _______________________________

Clue one: I am a protein in your blood.
Clue two: When I combine with oxygen, I turn blood red.
Clue three: When I am not combined with oxygen, I look purple or blue when you see me through your skin.

Name/Date _______________________________

Circulatory System 20

Match the numbers to the correct descriptions.

_______ 1. Amount of blood in a human body
_______ 2. How many days red blood cells live
_______ 3. Amount of red blood cells made each day
_______ 4. Percent of your blood that is red blood cells
_______ 5. Percent of your blood that is plasma

a. 55
b. $\frac{1}{2}$ cup
c. 100–120
d. 12 pints or 5–6 liters
e. 44

Human Body Warm-ups: Circulatory System

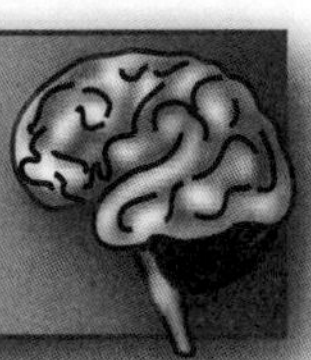

Name/Date ______________________

Circulatory System 21

Write "T" for true or "F" for false.

______ 1. White blood cells are made in the spleen and the lymph nodes.

______ 2. White blood cells have no nuclei.

______ 3. White blood cells look for germs to destroy.

______ 4. White blood cells make antibodies to fight off diseases.

Name/Date ______________________

Circulatory System 22

Number these steps in order to show what happens when you cut yourself.

______ a. Platelets use a protein called fibrin to help make a special net.

______ b. Platelets rush to the cut.

______ c. The net traps cells and makes a blood clot.

______ d. The blood clot gets large enough to stop the bleeding, and a scab forms.

______ e. You cut your finger.

Name/Date ______________________

Circulatory System 23

anemia   **coronary artery disease**   **stroke**

1. This happens when one or both coronary arteries become blocked with fatty deposits.

   ____

2. This occurs when a blood clot or air bubble gets stuck in an artery and blocks the supply of blood to a part of the brain. _______________________

3. This happens when there are not enough red blood cells or they don't work right, and the person gets too little oxygen. _______________________

Name/Date ______________________

Circulatory System 24

Explain what causes a bruise.

____

____

____

Name/Date ______________________

Circulatory System 25

1. What are the four types of human blood?

   ______ ______ ______ ______

2. Which blood type can donate to all other blood types? ______

3. Which blood type can only donate to its own blood type? ______

Human Body Warm-ups: Circulatory System

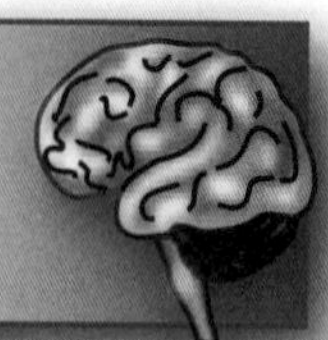

Name/Date ________________________

Circulatory System 26

Match these pulse rates with the activities.

______ 1. sleeping
______ 2. walking slowly
______ 3. running on a flat surface
______ 4. running up a hill

a. 120
b. 100
c. 85
d. 65

Name/Date ________________________

Circulatory System 27

contraction   relaxed   force
arteries   pressure

1. Blood pressure measures the ____________ the blood puts on the walls of the __________.
2. The top number measures the ____________ during a ______________ of the heart muscle.
3. The bottom number measures the pressure when the heart muscle is ______________.

Name/Date ________________________

Circulatory System 28

a. 600,000   b. 95,000   c. 4 billion   d. 65–75

______ 1. Length, in kilometers, of blood vessels in the body
______ 2. The average beats per minute of the heart
______ 3. Number of times the heart will beat in a lifetime
______ 4. Amount, in tons, of blood the heart will pump in a lifetime

---

Name/Date ________________________

Circulatory System 29

How is the circulatory system like a roadway?

____

____

____

Name/Date ________________________

Circulatory System 30

Fill in the blanks.

Blood flows from the right atrium through the t______________ valve into the right v____________, then out through the p____________ valve into the p____________ arteries and to the l____________. Then it goes from the p____________ veins into the left a____________ and through the m____________ valve into the left v____________. Then it travels out through the a____________ valve and to the body cells. The blood returns through the superior and inferior v____________.

Human Body Warm-ups: Digestive System

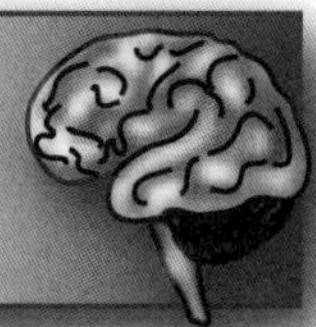

Name/Date ______________________

Digestive System 1

Label these parts of the digestive system on the diagram on page 37.

mouth	large intestine	salivary glands	esophagus
liver	stomach	gall bladder	rectum
small intestine		pancreas	

Name/Date ______________________

Digestive System 2

Add the missing vowels to find out three things our bodies use food for.

1. For ___ n ___ r g y
2. To provide the m ___ t ___ r ___ ___ l s to build our bodies
3. To provide the materials we need to r ___ b ___ ___ l d our bodies

Name/Date ______________________

Digestive System 3

Why is it necessary for the digestive system to break down the food you eat?

____

____

____

Name/Date ______________________

Digestive System 4

On your own paper, tell how each of these things in the mouth help in digestion.

1. teeth   2. tongue   3. saliva

Name/Date ______________________

____

Digestive System 5

Fill in the blanks.

peristalsis	esophagus
pepsin	gastric juices

1. The ______________________ is the long tube your food enters when you swallow.

2. ______________________ is the involuntary contracting and expanding of muscles in the esophagus that push the food to the stomach.

3. When food enters your stomach, it mixes with ______________________.

4. ______________________ is one of the enzymes that helps break down proteins and fats.

Human Body Warm-ups: Digestive System

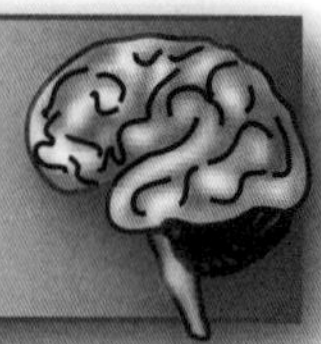

Name/Date _______________________

Digestive System 16

Write "T" for true or "F" for false.

______ 1. The appendix is located where the small intestine and large intestine meet.

______ 2. The appendix is a round, circular pouch.

______ 3. Scientists do not know the purpose of the appendix.

______ 4. The appendix can become infected and even burst. It then needs to be taken out.

Name/Date _______________________

Digestive System 17

Circle all of the words that are part of the digestive system.

liver	heart	mouth	pancreas
lungs	villi	rectum	appendix
sternum	stomach	pelvis	esophagus
saliva	peristalsis		gall bladder

Name/Date _______________________

Digestive System 18

a. salivary glands   b. sublingual glands

c. submaxillary glands   d. parotids

1. In your mouth is a set of six ______.

2. The largest of these glands is the ______, which are under the lower jaw.

3. The ______ are under the tongue.

4. The ______ are found in front of each ear.

Name/Date _______________________

Digestive System 19

Who am I? _______________________

Clue one: I am shaped sort of like a bunch of grapes.

Clue two: I make enzymes that help break down carbohydrates, proteins, and fats.

Clue three: My enzymes are sent to the small intestine.

Name/Date _______________________

Digestive System 20

Match the numbers to the correct descriptions.

______ 1. How many centimeters long the pancreas is   a. 2 to 3

______ 2. How many hours food stays in your stomach   b. 7

______ 3. How many meters long the small intestine is   c. 2 to 6

______ 4. How many pints of saliva you make each day   d. 20

Human Body Warm-ups: Digestive System

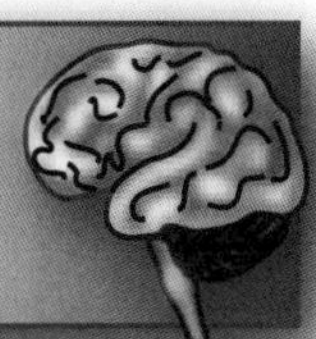

Name/Date ___________________________

Digestive System 21

Fill in the blanks.

pharynx   **trachea**   **esophagus**   **bolus**   **epiglottis**

When your food is chewed, it becomes a ball called a ___________________. This ball goes to the ___________________ in the back of the throat. The pharynx leads to two tubes. One is for air to travel down toward the lungs. This tube is called the ___________________. Food travels down the other tube, called the ___________________, to the stomach. A small flap called the ___________________ covers the trachea when you swallow so that food doesn't go into your lungs.

Name/Date ___________________________

Digestive System 22

1. When you swallow air and your stomach sends it back up your esophagus, this produces a ___________________.

2. When the diaphragm and stomach muscles contract and make jerking movements to push everything up through the esophagus, this is called ___________________.

Name/Date ___________________________

Digestive System 23

Check all that are functions of the liver.

______ 1. create bile to help break down fats

______ 2. separate the nutrients and send them where they are needed

______ 3. filter out things that are bad for you from the blood

______ 4. mix and churn the chyme

______ 5. help control blood sugar levels

Name/Date ___________________________

Digestive System 24

1. What part of the digestive system isn't working right if you have diabetes?

   ____

2. What part of the digestive system isn't working right if you have cirrhosis?

   ____

3. What part of the digestive system has problems if you have ulcers?

   ____

Name/Date ___________________________

Digestive System 25

What does *balanced nutrition* mean, and why is it important?

____

____

____

____

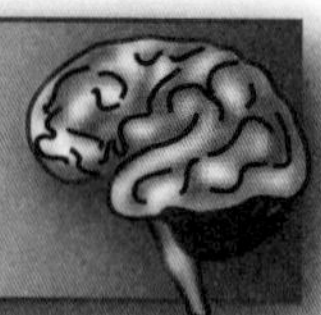

Human Body Warm-ups: Respiratory System

Name/Date ______________________

____

Respiratory System 1

Match each part of the nasal cavity with its purpose.

_____ 1. blood vessels

_____ 2. cilia

_____ 3. mucus

a. to filter the air you breathe in

b. to warm the air you breathe in

c. to moisten and filter the air you breathe in

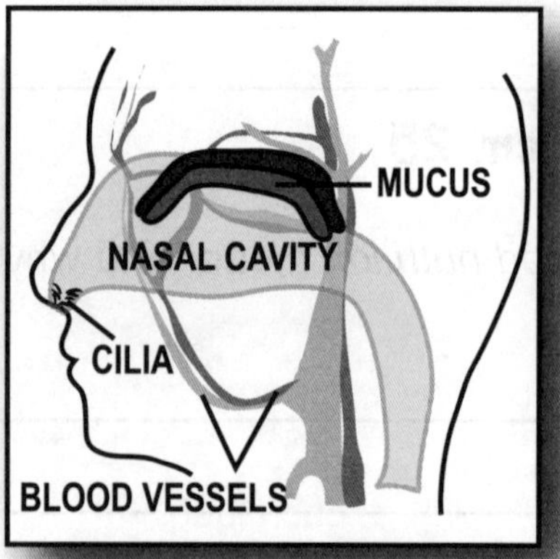

Name/Date ______________________

Respiratory System 2

Unscramble these sentences to describe the two jobs of the respiratory system. Write the corrected sentences on your own paper.

1. passes from air the blood The to oxygen respiratory the system.
2. respiratory removes wastes body system The gaseous the from.

Name/Date ______________________

Respiratory System 3

Why can people survive a few days without water and a week or more without food, but no more than a few minutes without oxygen? Write the answer on your own paper.

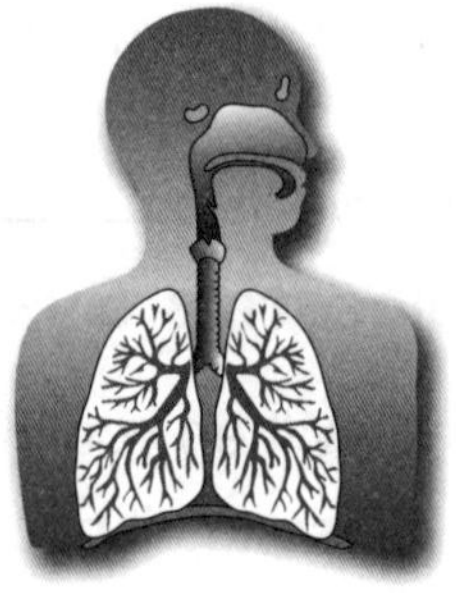

Name/Date ______________________

Respiratory System 4

Circle the words that are a part of the respiratory system.

pharynx	nose	liver	trachea
epiglottis	septum	lungs	bronchi
femur	larynx	alveoli	diaphragm

Name/Date ______________________

Respiratory System 5

Why do you think it might be better to breathe through your nose than your mouth?

____

____

____

Human Body Warm-ups: Respiratory System

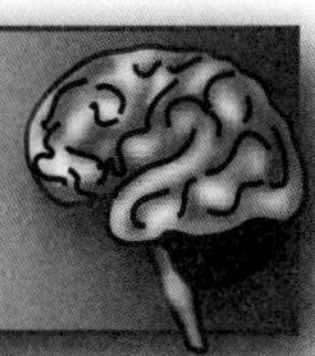

Name/Date ________________________

Respiratory System 6

What is the scientific name for each of these parts of the respiratory system?

1. nose ________________________

2. throat ________________________

3. windpipe ________________________

4. vocal cords ________________________

Name/Date ________________________

Respiratory System 7

larynx   cartilage   trachea   air   lungs

The ________________ is a tube about 12 inches long that leads to the ________________. It is held open by rings of C-shaped ________________. At the top of the trachea are the vocal cords, otherwise known as the ________________. Sound is made when ________________ passes over these folds of tissue.

Name/Date ________________________

Respiratory System 8

Number these in order from largest to smallest and then match to the correct definition.

Size		**Definition**
_____ a. alveoli	_____	d. two tubes that split off of the trachea
_____ b. bronchi	_____	e. tiny tubes that branch off of the bronchi
_____ c. bronchioles	_____	f. tiny clusters of air sacks that inflate

Name/Date ________________________

Respiratory System 9

What is the epiglottis, and what is its job?

____

____

____

Name/Date ________________________

Respiratory System 10

Write "T" for true or "F" for false.

_____ 1. Alveoli are tiny air sacs in clusters.

_____ 2. Alveoli are bigger than bronchioles.

_____ 3. Scientists believe there are about 300 million alveoli in each lung.

_____ 4. Alveoli expand like balloons when you breathe in and flatten when you breathe out.

Human Body Warm-ups:
Respiratory System

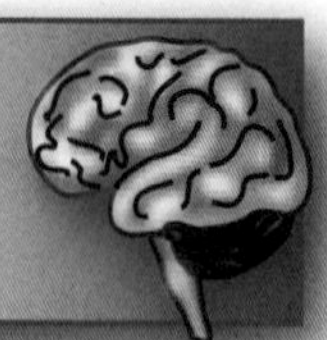

Name/Date _______________________

Respiratory System 11

muscle   **diaphragm**   **ribs**   **contracts**   **relaxes**   **chest**

The _______________ is a large sheet of _______________ that separates your _______________ from the lower part of your body. The diaphragm sits under your _______________. It _______________ and moves down when you breathe in, and it _______________ and moves up when you breathe out.

Name/Date _______________________

Respiratory System 12

Label these parts of the respiratory system on the diagram on page 38.

nasal cavity	**pharynx**	**larynx**
trachea	**alveoli**	**lung**
bronchial tube	**diaphragm**	**epiglottis**

Name/Date _______________________

Respiratory System 13

Answer these questions on your own paper.

1. How does the oxygen you breathe in get from your lungs to all the cells in your body?

2. How does the carbon dioxide waste get out?

Name/Date _______________________

Respiratory System 14

Number these steps in order of the sequence for respiration.

_____ a. Carbon dioxide is carried to the lungs.

_____ b. Oxygen is carried to the cells.

_____ c. Oxygen is inhaled.

_____ d. Carbon dioxide is exhaled.

_____ e. Oxygen and glucose combine to release energy.

Name/Date _______________________

Respiratory System 15

Match the numbers to the definitions.

1. We inhale and exhale about _____ times each day.
2. The trachea is about _____ inches long.
3. We have about _____ c-shaped cartilage rings holding the trachea open.
4. The air we breathe is about _____ percent oxygen.

a. 20
b. 20,000
c. 12
d. 16–20

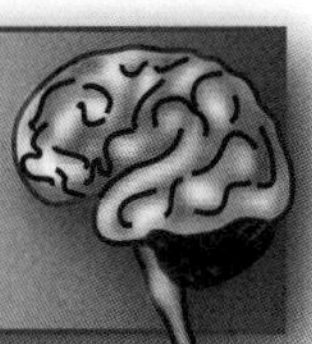

Human Body Warm-ups: Respiratory System

Name/Date ___________________________

Respiratory System 16

Place a check mark by each sentence that is true.

_______ 1. When you smoke, you inhale poisonous carbon monoxide.

_______ 2. When you smoke, carbon monoxide goes into the bloodstream and throughout your body.

_______ 3. Tar from cigarettes stays on the tissues in the lung when you smoke.

_______ 4. Smoking only harms your lungs.

Name/Date ___________________________

Respiratory System 17

Name two respiratory system disorders that are caused primarily from smoking.

____

____

Name/Date ___________________________

Respiratory System 18

Write "T" for true or "F" for false.

_______ 1. If you stretched out all your alveoli, they would cover an area as big as a tennis court.

_______ 2. Your left lung is slightly smaller than your right lung.

_______ 3. The muscles used in breathing are voluntary muscles.

Name/Date ___________________________

Respiratory System 19

Which person would you expect to have a greater lung capacity—a marathon runner or an average adult who smokes? Why?

____

____

____

____

Name/Date ___________________________

Respiratory System 20

Yawning **Snoring** **Hyperventilation**

1. ___________________________ occurs when you take in too much oxygen. It makes you dizzy.

2. ___________________________ happens when the soft palate in the back of your throat vibrates when you breathe deeply in your sleep.

3. ___________________________ forces your body to draw more oxygen into your lungs. It means you need more oxygen.

Human Body Warm-ups: Excretory System

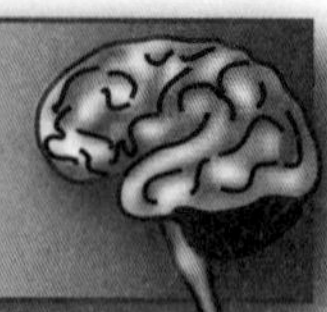

Name/Date _______________________

____

Excretory System 1

Fill in the blanks with the words below.

rectum

anus

large intestines

digestive

nutrients

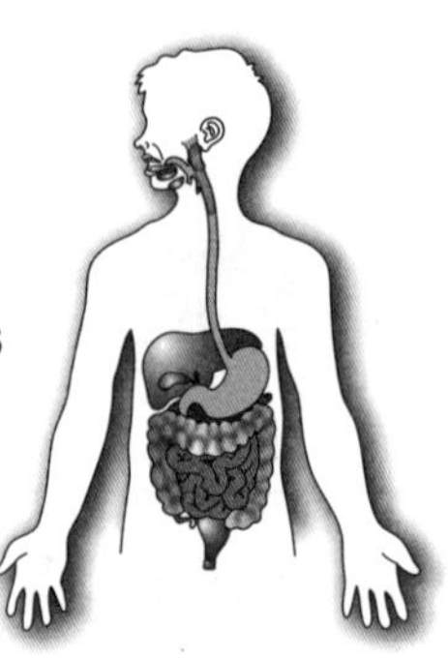

Solid food wastes

are removed by the

_______________________ system.

When _______________________

have been removed from the

food, the waste moves into the

_______________________.

There, water and salts are

removed, and the remainder is

stored in the _______________________

and expelled from the body

through the _______________________.

Name/Date _______________________

Excretory System 2

Name the three types of wastes that must be removed from your body.

1. S __ __ __ __ __
2. G __ __ __ __ __ __ __
3. L __ __ __ __ __ __

Name/Date _______________________

Excretory System 3

Match the type of waste with the system that removes it.

_______ 1. solid food wastes   a. urinary system

_______ 2. gaseous wastes   b. digestive system

_______ 3. liquid wastes   c. respiratory system

Name/Date _______________________

Excretory System 4

Answer this question on your own paper.

Describe how gaseous wastes are removed from the body through the respiratory system.

Name/Date _______________________

Excretory System 5

Label these parts on the diagram of the urinary system on page 39.

kidneys   **ureter**   **urethra**   **bladder**

Human Body Warm-ups: Excretory System

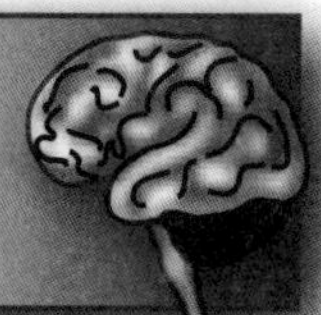

Name/Date _______________________________

Excretory System 6

1. How many kidneys do you normally have? _______

2. What are the tiny filtering units in the kidneys called? _______________________

3. What is their responsibility? _______________________ ____

Name/Date _______________________________

Excretory System 7

Unscramble these four things that are forced into collecting tubes as the blood travels through the nephrons (parts of which later become urine).

1. odof smeolleuc _______________________

2. tsasl _______   3. trawe _______   4. aeru _______

Name/Date _______________________________

Excretory System 8

Your kidneys clean all of your blood more than 50 times each day. Find out about how many minutes it takes to clean your blood by calculating how many minutes are in a 24-hour period and dividing that by 50.

Your blood is cleaned approximately every _______ minutes.

Name/Date _______________________________

Excretory System 9

What are we? _______________________

Clue one: We are two tubes connected to the kidneys.
Clue two: We are about 10–12 inches long.
Clue three: Urine from the kidneys travels through us on the way to the bladder.

Name/Date _______________________________

____

Excretory System 10

Write "T" for true or "F" for false.

_______ 1. The bladder sits above the kidneys.

_______ 2. The bladder is a muscular sac.

_______ 3. The bladder collects and holds urine until you urinate.

_______ 4. The bladder can hold one gallon of urine.

Human Body Warm-ups: Excretory System

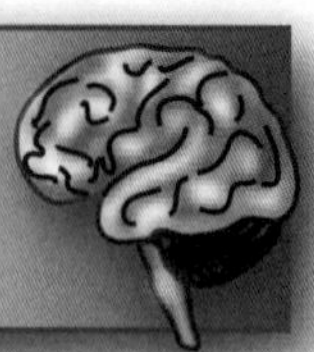

Name/Date ___________________

Excretory System 11

Why does the bladder have to be a stretchable muscular sac?

____

____

____

____

Name/Date ___________________

Excretory System 12

Fill in the blanks.

outside   urinary   bladder   kidneys

The last part of the urinary system is the urethra. It leads from the _______________ to the _______________ of the body. All together, the _______________, ureters, bladder, and urethra are called the _______________ tract.

Name/Date ___________________

Excretory System 13

Put a check by the sentences that are true.

_______ 1. Each kidney is about as big as a fist.

_______ 2. If your urine has protein in it, there might be a problem with your kidneys.

_______ 3. It is possible to live with just one kidney.

_______ 4. Your kidneys lie right beside your bladder.

Name/Date ___________________

Excretory System 14

What is dialysis?

____

____

____

Name/Date ___________________

Excretory System 15

Fill in the blanks.   **urea   wastes   cool off   salts   pores**

1. When you sweat, your body is trying to _______________.

2. When you sweat, your body is also getting rid of _______________.

3. When you sweat, the sweat moves from the glands through holes on your skin called _______________.

4. When the water in your sweat evaporates, the _______________ and _______________ remain on your skin until you wash them off.

 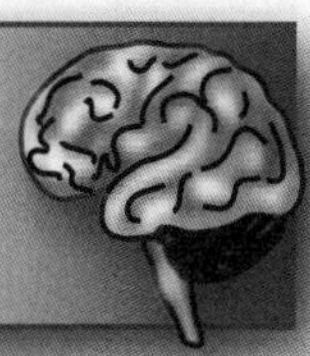

Human Body Warm-ups: Nervous System

Name/Date ____

Nervous System 1

The nervous system has five jobs. Fill in the blanks with the correct words.

respond   sense   controls   learning   memory   consciousness

1. To maintain your _______________________
2. To help you _______________________ to the senses
3. Coordinate what you _______________________ or feel
4. Responsible for _______________________ and _______________________
5. _______________________ the other body systems

Name/Date _______________________________________

Nervous System 2

List each item in the correct category.

**cranial nerves   brain   spinal nerves
spinal cord**

central nervous system: _______________________

____

peripheral nervous system: _______________________

Name/Date _______________________________________

Nervous System 3

In what way does the skeletal system help the nervous system?

____

____

____

____

Name/Date _______________________________________

Nervous System 4

Label these parts of the diagram of a neuron.

dendrite   axon   nucleus   cell body

Name/Date _______________________________________

Nervous System 5

Draw lines to match the terms and definitions.

1. dendrites   a. the space between two neurons
2. axons   b. receive messages from other neurons
3. synapse   c. send messages to other neurons
4. nucleus   d. the control center of the neuron

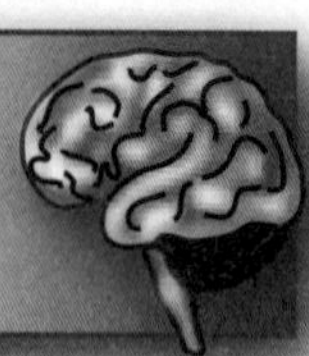

Human Body Warm-ups: Nervous System

Name/Date _______________________

Nervous System 6

a. interphase neurons   b. sensory neurons
c. motor neurons

1. Which type of neuron gathers information and sends it to your brain or spinal cord? _______

2. Which type of neuron serves as a link between the other types of neurons? _______

3. Which kind of neuron carries information to muscles or glands? _______

Name/Date _______________________

Nervous System 7

Put a check mark beside the actions that are reflexes.

_____   1. blinking your eyes

_____   2. standing up

_____   3. pulling your hand away from a hot stove

_____   4. chewing your food

Name/Date _______________________

Nervous System 8

Change the underlined words to make the information correct.

Neurons <u>do</u> touch each other. There is an empty space between neurons called a <u>dendrite</u>. When an axon of one neuron sends information to the <u>synapse</u> of another neuron, it uses special <u>fibers</u> to send the information. The chemicals travel from the <u>nucleus</u>, through the synapse and to the dendrite of the next neuron, without actually touching it.

Name/Date _______________________

Nervous System 9

Write "T" for true or "F" for false.

_____   1. The brain is protected by the skull.

_____   2. The average adult brain weighs about 10 pounds.

_____   3. The brain contains 100 billion neurons.

_____   4. The brain receives 100 million messages every second.

Name/Date _______________________

Nervous System 10

Unscramble the three parts of the brain. Then label them on the diagram.

1. bmceurer

2. mleeecrblu

3. nrabi mset

Human Body Warm-ups: Nervous System

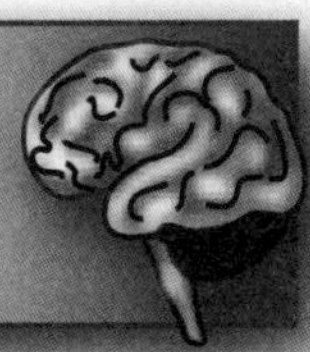

Name/Date _______________________

Nervous System 11

List which of the five sense organs (eyes, ears, tongue, nose, skin) would be stimulated by each stimulus. (Choose the main one stimulated if there is more than one.)

1. Looking at a rainbow _______________
2. Stepping on a tack _______________
3. A balloon popping _______________
4. Freshly baked bread _______________
5. Eating a cookie _______________
6. Sucking a peppermint stick _______________
7. Listening to a rock song _______________
8. A dead skunk _______________
9. A laser show _______________
10. Feeling sandpaper _______________

Name/Date _______________________

Nervous System 12

1. Which area of the brain controls body functions necessary for survival, such as your breathing, your heartbeat, and blood pressure? _______________
2. Which area of the brain controls your movements and balance? _______________
3. Which area of the brain controls your thinking, memory, and learning? _______________

Name/Date _______________________

Nervous System 13

1. Tiny hairs inside the nose that filter the air are called c _ _ _ _ .
2. The sticky substance inside the nose that warms the air and traps dust is called m _ _ _ _ .
3. The two openings at the bottom of the nose are called n _ _ _ _ _ _ _ .

Name/Date _______________________

Nervous System 14

Circle all the words that are part of the eye.

iris   **pupil**   **cochlea**   **cones**

lens   **rods**   **cilia**   **cornea**

optic nerve   **retina**

Name/Date _______________________

Nervous System 15

Place a check mark by each sentence that is correct.

_____ 1. The cochlea carries sound waves to the eardrum.
_____ 2. The anvil, hammer, and stirrup are tiny bones through which vibrations pass.
_____ 3. Parts of the inner ear help us maintain our balance.

Human Body Warm-ups: Nervous System

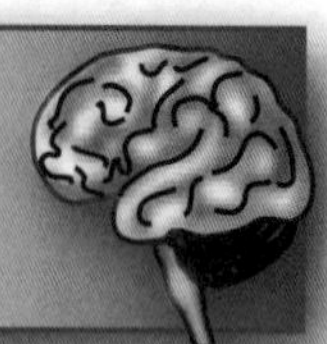

Name/Date _______________________

Nervous System 16

Label these parts of the eye.

optic nerve
lens
retina
iris
cornea
pupil

Name/Date _______________________

Nervous System 17

What am I? _______________________

Clue one: I am the largest organ of the body.

Clue two: I have two layers—the epidermis and the dermis.

Clue three: My outer cells are mostly dead, and millions of them get rubbed off each day.

Name/Date _______________________

Nervous System 18

Fill in the blanks.

keratin   hair follicles   melanin   pores

1. A brown pigment that gives color to the skin _______________________

2. A protein that makes the skin waterproof _______________________

3. Sweat or perspiration leaves the skin through these. _______________________

4. Hair grows from these dents in the skin. _______________________

Name/Date _______________________

Nervous System 19

Number these steps in order to explain how our sense of taste works.

____ a. Receptor cells send signals to the brain's taste center for identification.

____ b. The dissolved food enters openings in the taste buds called taste pores.

____ c. The part of food that carries flavor is dissolved in saliva.

____ d. Food is chewed and mixed with saliva.

Name/Date _______________________

Nervous System 20

Label the part of the tongue where each taste is detected.

salty

sweet

sour

bitter

Human Body Warm-ups: Endocrine System

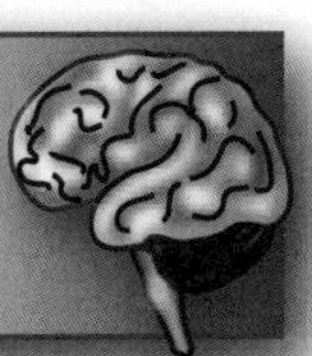

Name/Date _______________________

Endocrine System 1

a. metabolism b. thyroxine   c. chemical
d. thyroid   e. hormone

The _______ is a gland found in the throat that releases the _______ called _______. This hormone controls your body's _______. The metabolism is all the _______ reactions that take place in your body.

Name/Date _______________________

Endocrine System 2

Write "T" for true or "F" for false.

_______ 1. The adrenal glands are behind the kidneys.

_______ 2. Adrenaline is the "fight or flight" hormone.

_______ 3. An adrenal gland makes more than 30 hormones.

_______ 4. You have one adrenal gland in your body.

Name/Date _______________________

Endocrine System 3

Number these parts of the endocrine system in order according to where they are in the body (#1 highest to #4 lowest).

_______ a. adrenal glands

_______ b. pituitary gland

_______ c. pancreas

_______ d. thyroid and parathyroids

Name/Date _______________________

Endocrine System 4

1. Which gland is part of both the endocrine system and the digestive system?

   ____

2. Which gland is responsible for how fast your bones, muscles, and organs grow?

   ____

3. Which gland is responsible for how fast you use up the food you eat?

   ____

Name/Date _______________________

Endocrine System 5

Draw lines to match the item to its definition.

1. Releases thyroxine to control metabolism
2. Controls salt in the blood and the balance of water
3. Makes enzymes that aid in digestion
4. Master gland that controls the other glands
5. Release hormones to control the amount of phosphate and calcium in the blood

a. pituitary gland
b. pancreas
c. thyroid
d. parathyroids
e. adrenal glands

 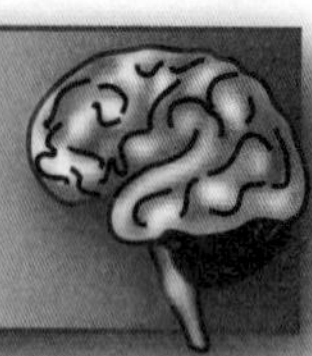

Human Body Warm-ups:
Skeletal System Diagram

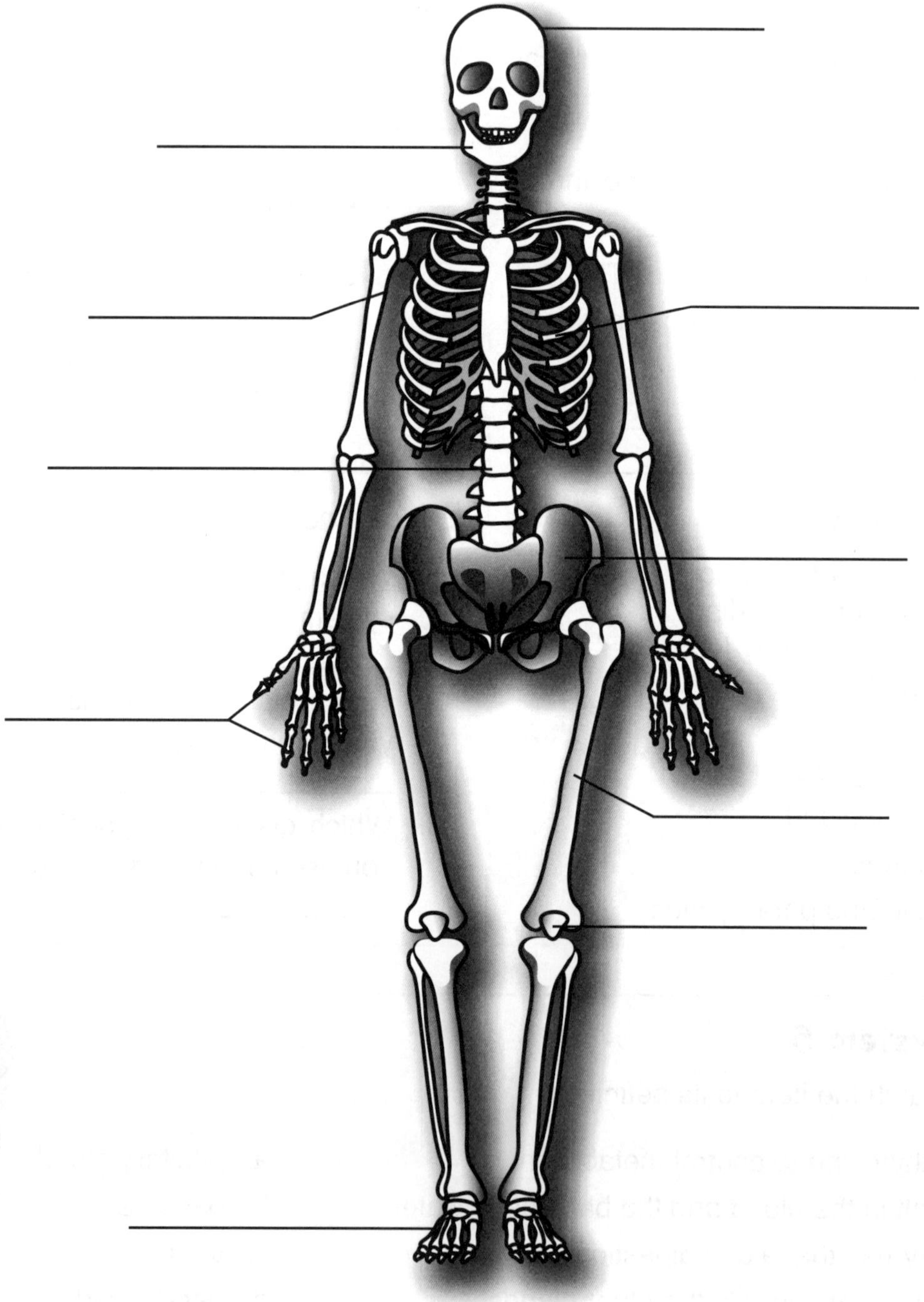

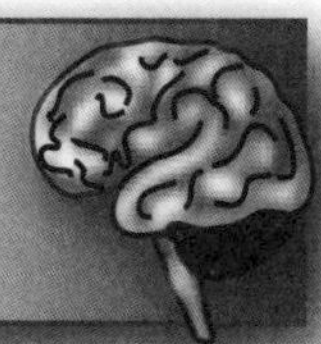

Human Body Warm-ups:
Heart Diagram

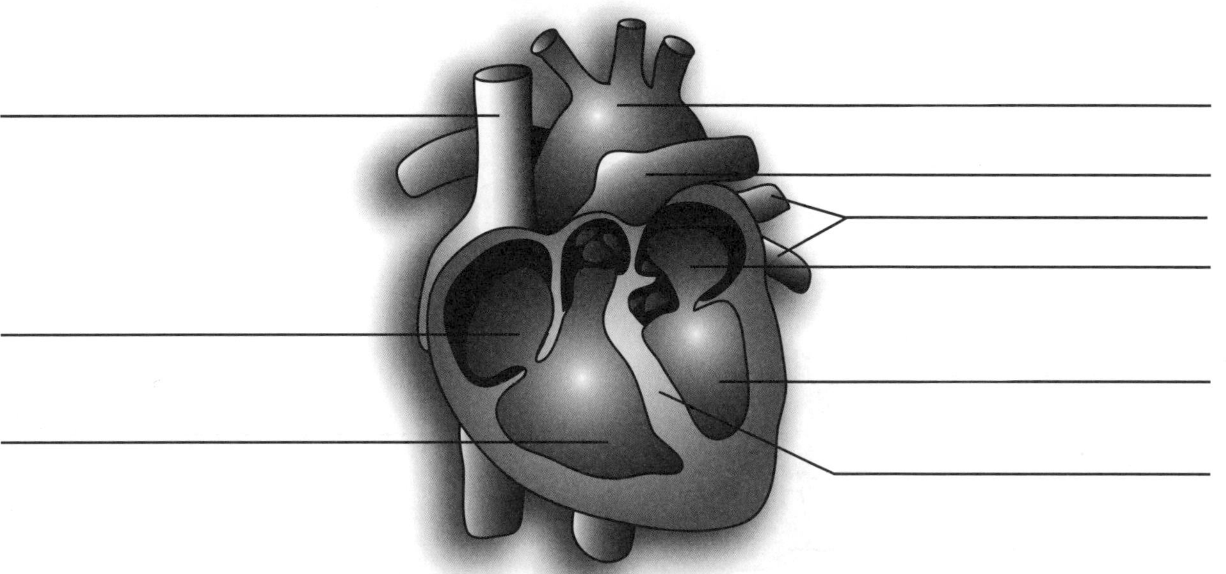

Digestive System Diagram

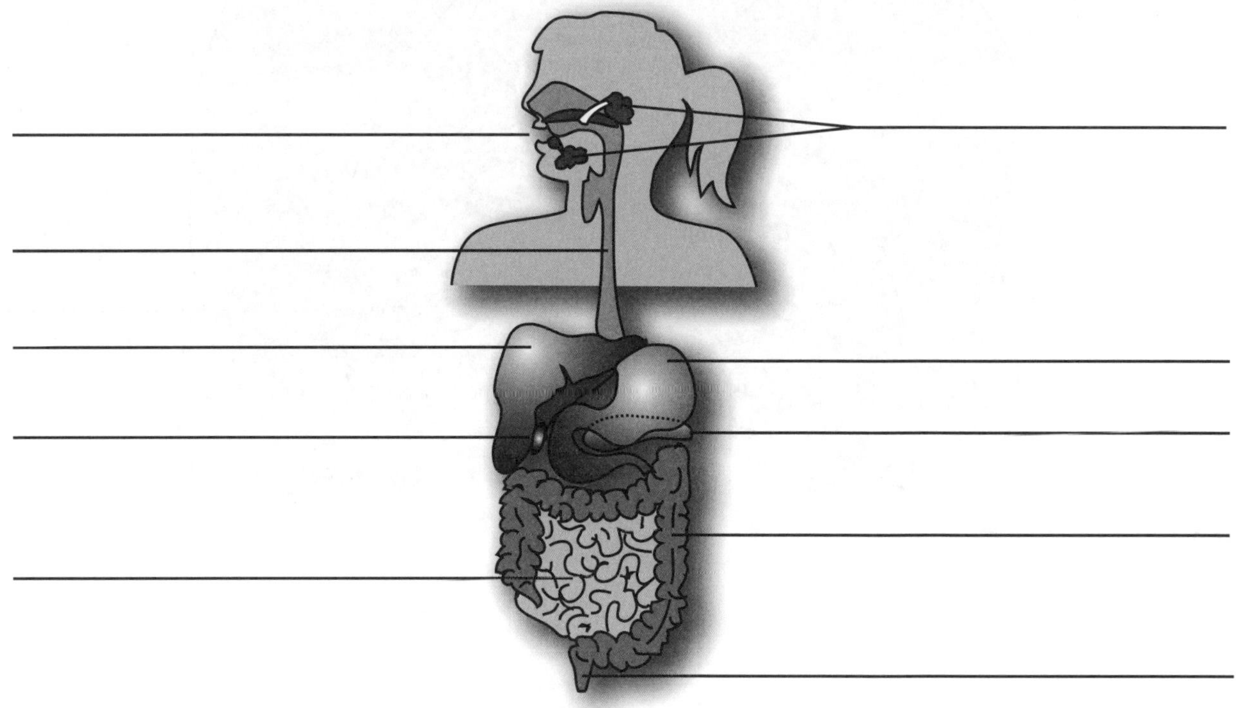

Human Body Warm-ups:
Respiratory System Diagram

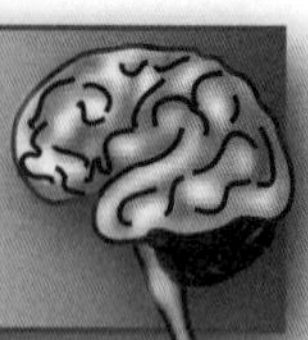

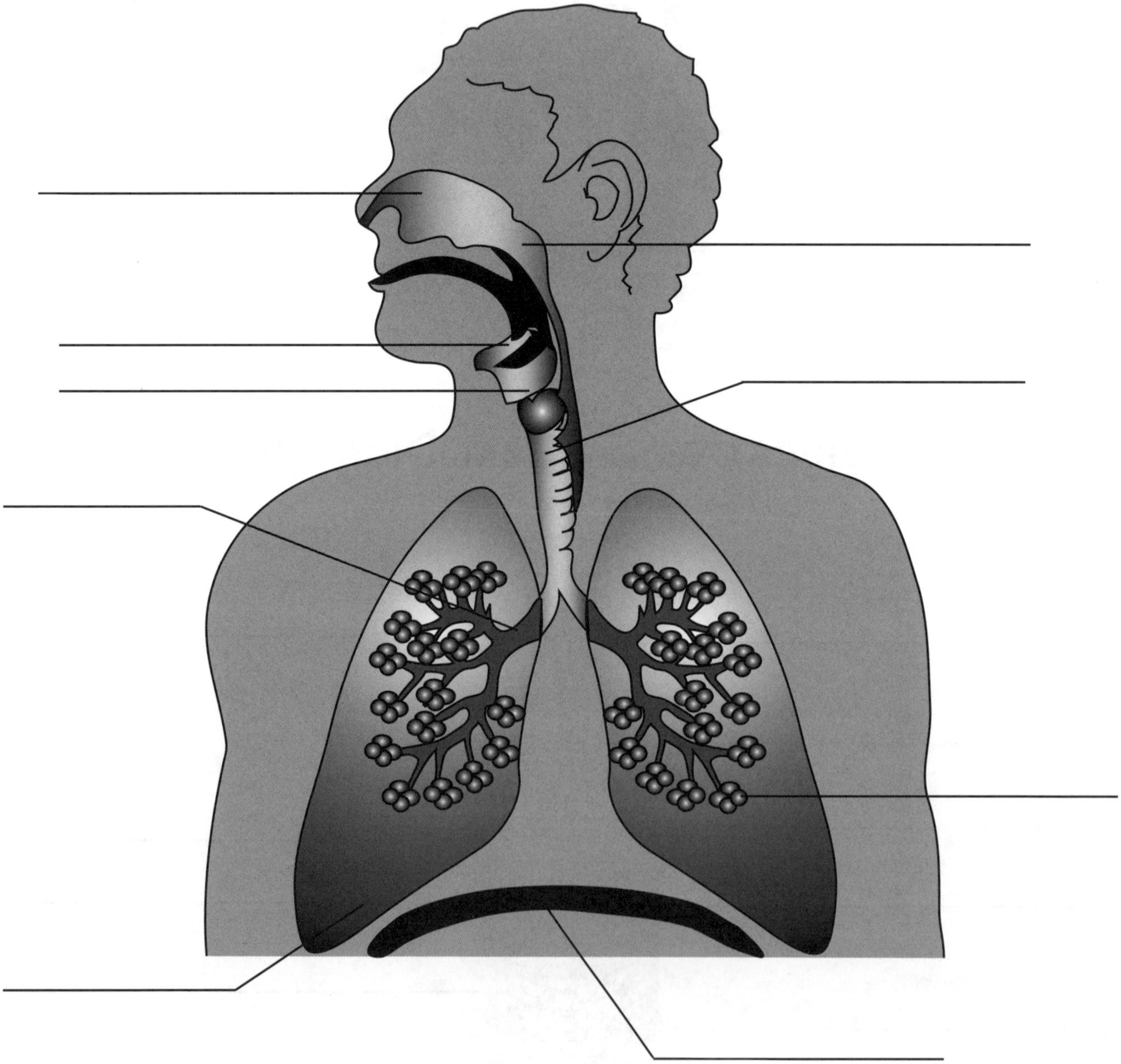

Human Body Warm-ups:
Urinary System Diagram

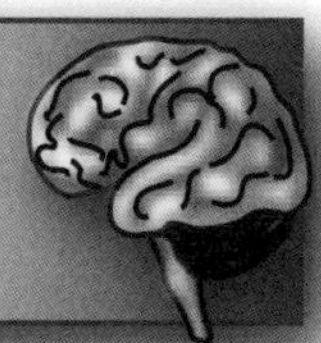

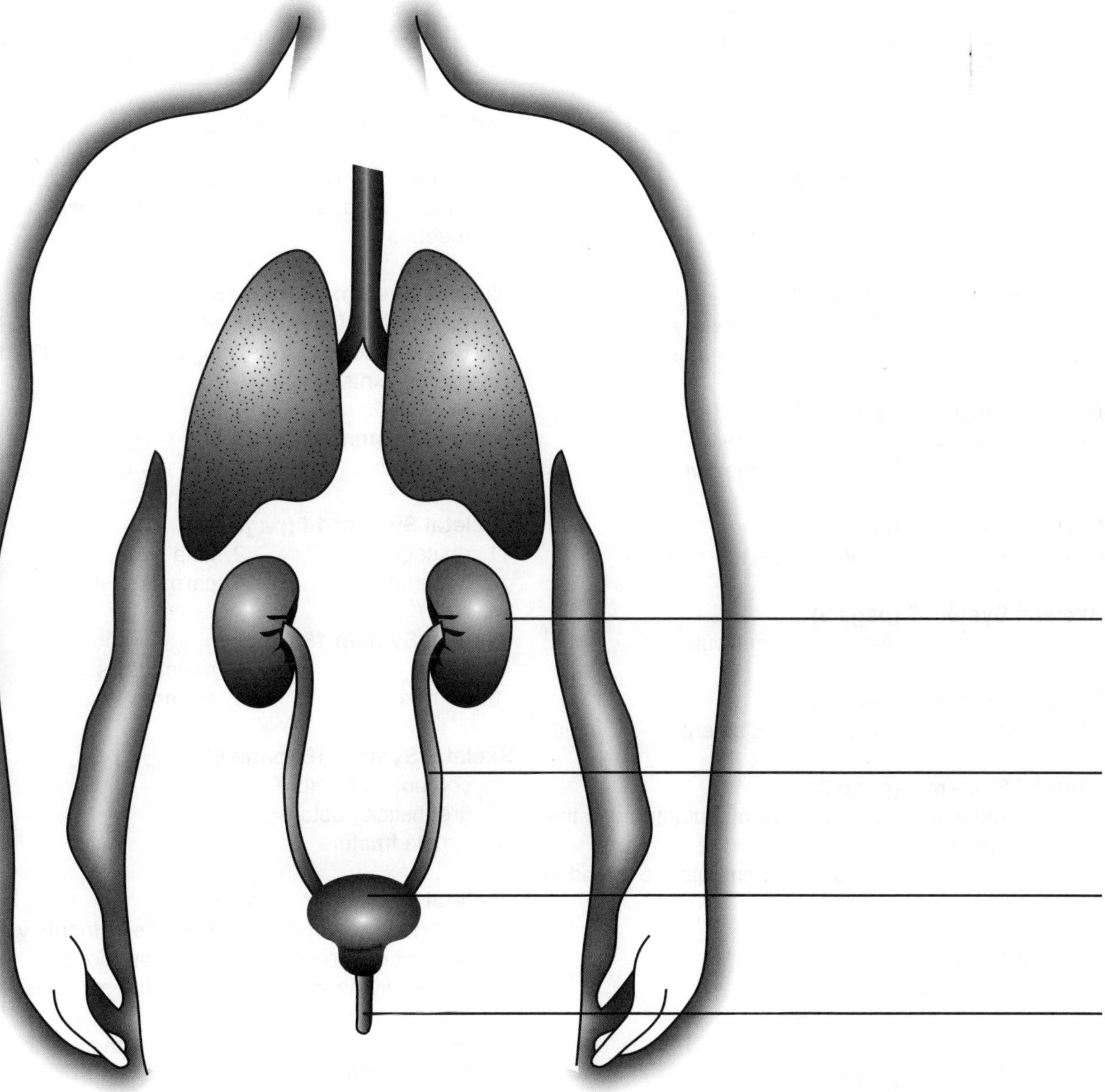

Answer Keys

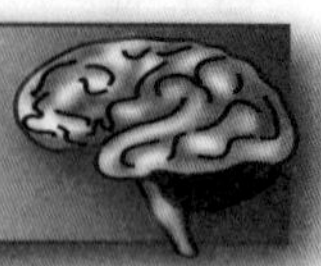

Body Organization 1 (page 2)
1. c   2. d   3. a   4. b

Body Organization 2 (page 2)

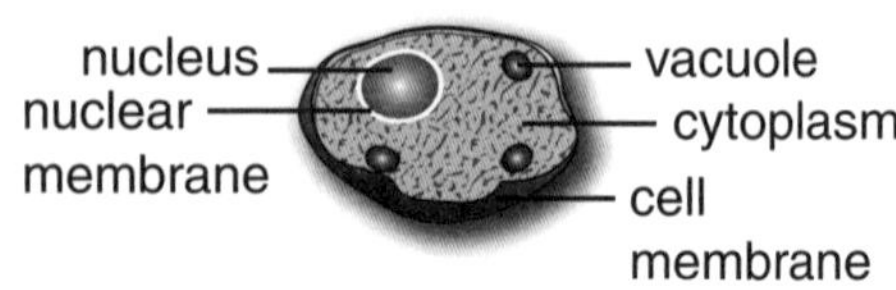

Body Organization 3 (page 2)
1.   2. S   3. T   4. S   5. T
6.   7. O   8. T   9. S   10. O

Body Organization 4 (page 2)
1. circulatory   2. excretory
3. skeletal   4. respiratory

Body Organization 5 (page 2)
1. muscular   2. nervous
3. endocrine   4. digestive

Skeletal System 1 (page 3)
brain, heart, lungs (Other answers are possible.)

Skeletal System 2 (page 3)
1. marrow   2. Fat   3. muscular

Skeletal System 3 (page 3)
1. bones   2. cartilage   3. ligaments   4. joints

Skeletal System 4 (page 3)
1. Red and white blood cells are manufactured in the red bone marrow.
2. Fat cells, calcium, and other minerals are stored in the yellow bone marrow.

Skeletal System 5 (page 3)
1. Yes   2. No   3. Yes
4. Yes   5. No   6. Yes

Skeletal System 6 (page 4)
1. T   2. T   3. F   4. T   5. F

Skeletal System 7 (page 4)
1. c   2. a   3. b

Skeletal System 8 (page 4)
1. jawbone   2. shoulder blade
3. skull   4. breastbone
5. shinbone/lower leg bone

Skeletal System 9 (page 4)
1. finger/toe bones   2. hip bones
3. kneecap   4. upper arm bone
5. backbone

Skeletal System 10 (page 4)
1. nose   2. ears   3. ends of bones

Skeletal System 11 (page 5)
1. Ligaments need to be stretchy so that they will not tear as they work with muscles to move the body.
2. Cartilage absorbs the shocks when two bones meet.

Skeletal System 12 (page 5)
1. Fixed joints (such as the skull)
2. Ball-and-socket joints, hinged joints, pivot joints, gliding joints

Skeletal System 13 (page 5)
1. d   2. b   3. e   4. a   5. c

Skeletal System 14 (page 5)
1. rib cage   2. ulna
3. cranium   4. carpals

Skeletal System 15 (page 5)
1. femur   2. metatarsals
3. humerus   4. sternum

Skeletal System 16 (page 6)
1. compound fracture
2. greenstick fracture
3. simple fracture

Skeletal System 17 (page 6)
1. You need a proper diet to get the nutrients your body needs to grow correctly. Your bones especially need calcium and other minerals to grow.
2. Ossification is the process where the cartilage changes into bone.

Skeletal System 18 (page 6)
a. 3   b. 1   c. 2   d. 4

Skeletal System 19 (page 6)
Answers will vary.

Skeletal System 20 (page 6)
1. T   2. T   3. T   4. F

Skeletal System 21 (page 7)
1. cervical   2. coccygeal   3. thoracic
4. lumbar   5. sacral

Skeletal System 22 (page 7)
1. patella   2. radius   3. fibula
4. sternum

Skeletal System 23 (page 7)
1. F   2. T   3. T   4. F   5. F

Skeletal System 24 (page 7)

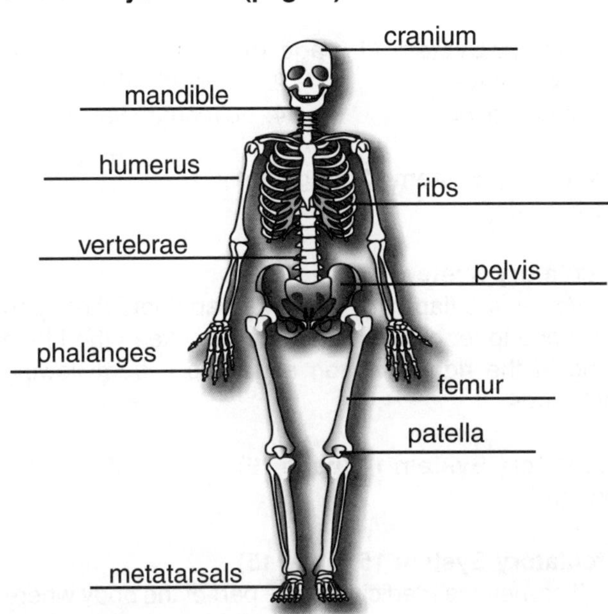

Skeletal System 25 (page 7)
1 cranium   2 clavicle   3 ribs
4 radius   5 carpals   6 femur
7 tibia   8 metatarsals

Muscular System 1 (page 8)
1. actin, myosin   2. slide

Muscular System 2 (page 8)
1. 44 lbs   2. 28 lbs.

Muscular System 3 (page 8)
1. T   2. F   3. T   4. T

Muscular System 4 (page 8)
1. muscles   2. tendons   3. ligaments

Muscular System 5 (page 8)
1. 650   2. True   3. muscle cell

Muscular System 6 (page 9)
Voluntary muscles you consciously decide to move.
    Example: biceps/arm muscle

Involuntary muscles are those that move automatically.
    Example: heart muscle

Muscular System 7 (page 9)
1. c   2. a   3. b

Muscular System 8 (page 9)
1. I   2. V   3. V   4. V
5. V   6. I   7. I   8. V
Diaphragm; You can breathe voluntarily, but you also breathe involuntarily.

Muscular System 9 (page 9)
1. C   2. S   3. V   4. S   5. V

Muscular System 10 (page 9)
1. F   2. T   3. T   4. T

Muscular System 11 (page 10)
1. contract, cramp
2. exercise, oxygen
3. overstretched, sprain

Muscular System 12 (page 10)
a. 3   b. 1   c. 2   d. 4

Muscular System 13 (page 10)
1. Yes   2. No   3. Yes   4. Yes

Muscular System 14 (page 10)
The diaphragm

Muscular System 15 (page 10)
1. It shapes and defines them.
2. It makes the heart bigger, stronger, and more efficient by making it pump harder and faster.

Muscular System 16 (page 11)
1. T   2. F   3. F   4. T

Muscular System 17 (page 11)
1. bone, bone   2. muscle, bone

Muscular System 18 (page 11)
1. flexor   2. extensor

Muscular System 19 (page 11)
1. d   2. b   3. a   4. c

Muscular System 20 (page 11)
Arm & Hand: pectoral, triceps, deltoid
Leg & Foot: quadriceps, soleus, tibialis
Head & Trunk: masseter, intercostals, gluteus maximus

Muscular System 21 (page 12)
To provide the nutrients required for growth, to strengthen the muscles, and to allow them to rebuild

Muscular System 22 (page 12)
oxygen, lactic, acid

Muscular System 23 (page 12)
1. When muscles reduce in size due to lack of use
2. When muscles increase in size due to overuse

Muscular System 24 (page 12)
1. skeletal   2. involuntary   3. smooth

Muscular System 25 (page 12)
1. ligaments   2. voluntary   3. tendons

Circulatory System 1 (page 13)
1. The circulatory system delivers food, water, and oxygen to every cell in the body.
2. The circulatory system removes waste from the cells.

Circulatory System 2 (page 13)
Numbers 1, 3, and 4 should be checked.

Circulatory System 3 (page 13)
1. heart: pumps blood
2. blood vessels: carry blood from the heart to all parts of the body.

Circulatory System 4 (page 13)
1. T   2. F   3. F   4. F

Circulatory System 5 (page 13)
These words should be circled: platelets, aorta, plasma, heart, blood, artery, veins, valves, oxygen, ventricle, capillaries

Circulatory System 6 (page 14)
pumps, lungs, oxygen, body, cells

Circulatory System 7 (page 14)

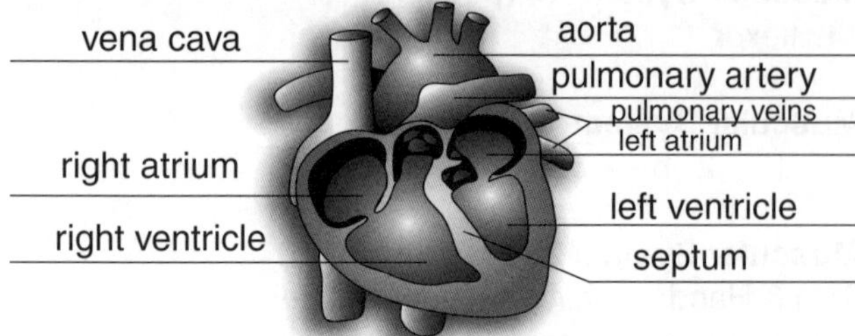

Circulatory System 8 (page 14)
1. c   2. a   3. b   4. d

Circulatory System 9 (page 14)
a. 2: carry blood back to the heart
b. 1: connect arteries with veins
c. 3: carry blood away from the heart

Circulatory System 10 (page 14)
1. Because the capillaries move up near the surface of the skin so the heat can be released. This gives the skin a rosy glow.
2. The capillaries move deep down under the skin to stay as close as possible to the important organs. This causes the surface of the skin to look pale.

Circulatory System 11 (page 15)
1. aortic valve   2. tricuspid valve
3. mitral valve   4. pulmonary valve

Circulatory System 12 (page 15)
1. F   2. T   3. F   4. T

Circulatory System 13 (page 15)
Valves are flaps that work like trap doors that open and close to let blood in and out. They keep the blood going in the right direction and keep it from flowing backwards.

Circulatory System 14 (page 15)
septum

Circulatory System 15 (page 15)
It carries the medicine to the part of the body where it is needed.

Circulatory System 16 (page 16)
1. plasma/platelets   2. red blood cells
3. white blood cells   4. platelets/plasma

Circulatory System 17 (page 16)
Sentences 1, 2, and 4 should be circled.

Circulatory System 18 (page 16)
oxygen, carbon dioxide, lungs, bone marrow, nucleus

Circulatory System 19 (page 16)
hemoglobin

Circulatory System 20 (page 16)
1. d   2. c   3. b   4. e   5. a

Circulatory System 21 (page 17)
1. T   2. F   3. T   4. T

Circulatory System 22 (page 17)
a. 3 b. 2 c. 4 d. 5 e. 1

Circulatory System 23 (page 17)
1. coronary artery disease
2. stroke
3. anemia

Circulatory System 24 (page 17)
When you hit or bump something, the capillaries break and you bleed a little under the skin.

Circulatory System 25 (page 17)
1. A, B, AB, O (in any order)
2. O   3. AB

Circulatory System 26 (page 18)
1. d   2. c   3. b   4. a

Circulatory System 27 (page 18)
1. force, arteries
2. pressure, contraction
3. relaxed

Circulatory System 28 (page 18)
1. b   2. d   3. c   4. a

Circulatory System 29 (page 18)
The blood vessels are like roads that take you to your destination with routes to get wherever you need to go. (Answers will vary.)

Circulatory System 30 (page 18)
tricuspid, ventricle, pulmonary, pulmonary, lungs, pulmonary, atrium, mitral, ventricle, aortic, vena cava

Digestive System 1 (page 19)

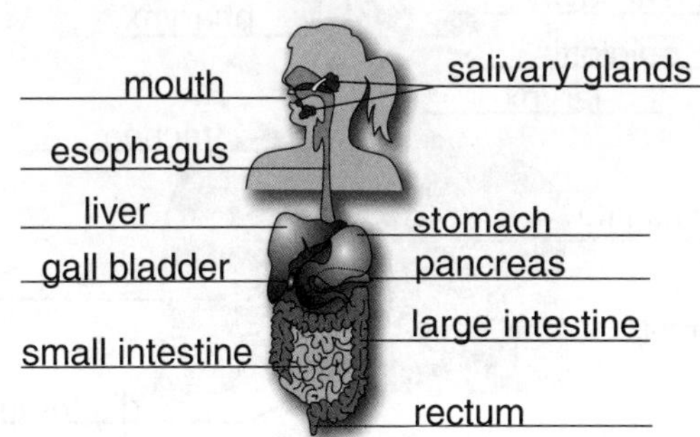

Digestive System 2 (page 19)
1. energy   2. materials   3. rebuild

Digestive System 3 (page 19)
So that the food is in small enough pieces so the nutrients can reach the cells where they are needed

Digestive System 4 (page 19)
1. Teeth: cut, grind, and chop the food into small pieces
2. Tongue: helps break the food apart and push it toward the esophagus for swallowing
3. Saliva: mixes with the food to begin a chemical breakdown of the food

Digestive System 5 (page 19)
1. esophagus   2. Peristalsis
3. gastric juices   4. Pepsin

Digestive System 6 (page 20)
1. Mechanical Digestion: the physical changes that happen to the food; the movement of the food through the digestive system
2. Chemical Digestion: the chemical changes that happen to the food we eat

Digestive System 7 (page 20)
1. fats   2. enzymes
3. proteins   4. acids
5. carbohydrates   6. bases

Digestive System 8 (page 20)
1. M   2. C   3. M   4. C   5. M

Digestive System 9 (page 20)
1. There is a mucus lining the stomach that protects its walls.
2. Chyme is the fluid when the food and gastric juices are fully mixed.

Digestive System 10 (page 20)
1. d   2. c   3. b   4. a

Digestive System 11 (page 21)
1. enamel
2. dentin
3. pulp

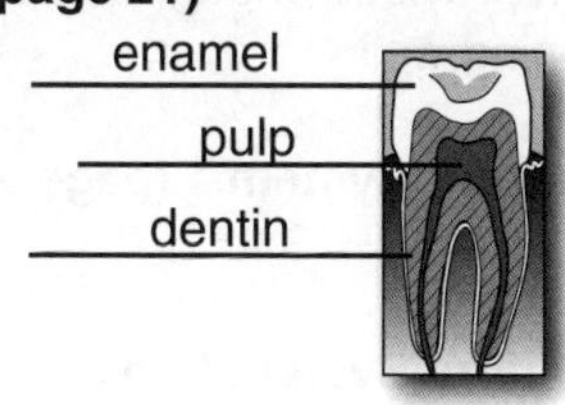

Digestive System 12 (page 21)
1. duodenum   2. jejunum   3. ilium

Digestive System 13 (page 21)
1. pancreas
2. Bile, liver, gall bladder
3. peristalsis

Digestive System 14 (page 21)
villi

Digestive System 15 (page 21)
To remove water and salts from the food waste product and prepare it to leave the body

Digestive System 16 (page 22)
1. T   2. F   3. T   4. T

Digestive System 17 (page 22)
These words should be circled: liver, villi, rectum, esophagus, mouth, appendix, saliva, pancreas, peristalsis, stomach, gall bladder

Digestive System 18 (page 22)
1. a   2. c   3. b   4. d

Digestive System 19 (page 22)
pancreas

Digestive System 20 (page 22)
1. d   2. c   3. b   4. a

Digestive System 21 (page 23)
bolus, pharynx, trachea, esophagus, epiglottis

Digestive System 22 (page 23)
1. burp/belch   2. vomiting

Digestive System 23 (page 23)
Sentences 1, 2, 3, and 5 should be checked.

Digestive System 24 (page 23)
1. pancreas   2. liver   3. stomach

Digestive System 25 (page 23)
Balanced nutrition means eating from all the different food groups in proper amounts. It is important because it provides enough fuel for the body and keeps it functioning well.

Respiratory System 1 (page 24)
1. b   2. a   3. c

Respiratory System 2 (page 24)
1. The respiratory system passes oxygen from the air to the blood.
2. The respiratory system removes gaseous wastes from the body.

Respiratory System 3 (page 24)
Our bodies are able to store some food and water to use in times when we can't get any, but our bodies cannot store any oxygen.

Respiratory System 4 (page 24)
The following words should be circled: pharynx, nose, trachea, epiglottis, lungs, bronchi, larynx, alveoli, diaphragm

Respiratory System 5 (page 24)
It is better to breathe through the nose because the nose has cilia and mucus to help filter, clean, and moisten the air we breathe.

Respiratory System 6 (page 25)
1. nasal cavity   2. pharynx
3. trachea   4. larynx

Respiratory System 7 (page 25)
trachea, lungs, cartilage, larynx, air

Respiratory System 8 (page 25)
a. 3, f   b. 1, d   c. 2, e

Respiratory System 9 (page 25)
The epiglottis is a flap that covers the trachea when you swallow, so that food will not go down it into the lungs.

Respiratory System 10 (page 25)
1. T   2. F   3. T   4. T

Respiratory System 11 (page 26)
diaphragm, muscle, chest, ribs, contracts, relaxes

Respiratory System 12 (page 26)

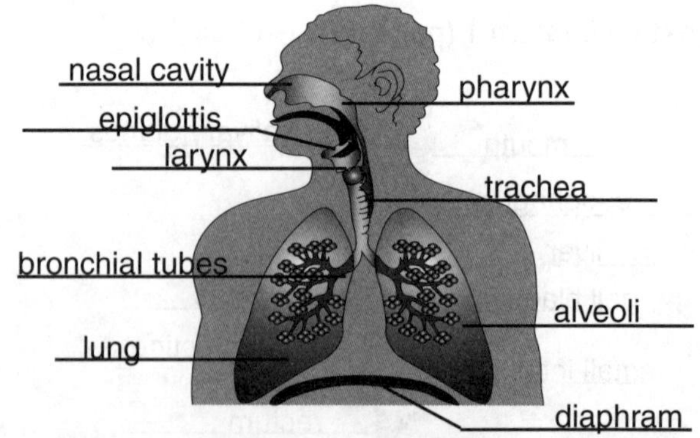

Respiratory System 13 (page 26)
1. The oxygen is absorbed from the alveoli into the capillaries at the end of the blood vessels, and then the circulatory system delivers it to the cells.
2. The carbon dioxide is absorbed from the capillaries into the alveoli and released in the air we breathe out.

Respiratory System 14 (page 26)
a. 4   b. 2   c. 1   d. 5   e. 3

Respiratory System 15 (page 26)
1. b   2. c   3. d   4. a

Respiratory System 16 (page 27)
Sentences 1, 2, and 3 should be checked.

Respiratory System17 (page 27)
lung cancer, emphysema (or any other respiratory disorder affected by smoking)

Respiratory System 18 (page 27)
1. T   2. T   3. F

Respiratory System 19 (page 27)
A marathon runner, because he exercises his lungs as he runs and because smoking would decrease the lung capacity of the smoker

Respiratory System 20 (page 27)
1. Hyperventilation   2. Snoring   3. Yawning

Excretory System 1 (page 28)
digestive, nutrients, large intestines, rectum, anus

Excretory System 2 (page 28)
1. solid   2. gaseous   3. liquid

Excretory System 3 (page 28)
1. b   2. c   3. a

Excretory System 4 (page 28)
Gaseous wastes are removed when the carbon dioxide waste from the cells is carried by the circulatory system to the lungs, where it is absorbed by the alveoli and then released when we exhale.

Excretory System 5 (page 28)

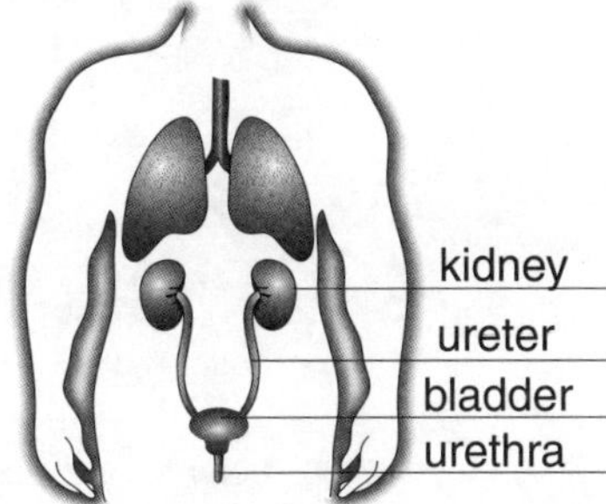

Excretory System 6 (page 29)
1. 2   2. nephrons
3. to clean the blood by filtering out the unnecessary materials

Excretory System 7 (page 29)
1. food molecules   2. salts
3. water   4. urea

Excretory System 8 (page 29)
28.8 minutes (between 25–30 minutes)

Excretory System 9 (page 29)
ureters

Excretory System 10 (page 29)
1. F   2. T   3. T   4. F

Excretory System 11 (page 30)
The bladder must stretch and get bigger as it fills up with urine. Then, when you urinate and the urine is released, the bladder needs to shrink back down to its original size.

Excretory System 12 (page 30)
bladder, outside, kidneys, urinary

Excretory System 13 (page 30)
Sentences 1, 2, and 3 should be checked.

Excretory System 14 (page 30)
Dialysis is the process where a special machine is used to clean the blood if the kidneys don't work. Blood travels through the machine, is filtered, and then travels back into the body.

Excretory System 15 (page 30)
1. cool off   2. wastes
3. pores   4. salts/urea

Nervous System 1 (page 31)
1. consciousness   2. respond
3. sense   4. learning/memory
5. Controls

Nervous System 2 (page 31)
Under central nervous system: brain, spinal cord
Under peripheral nervous system: cranial nerves, spinal nerves

Nervous System 3 (page 31)
The skull protects the brain and the vertebrae protect the spinal cord.

Nervous System 4 (page 31)

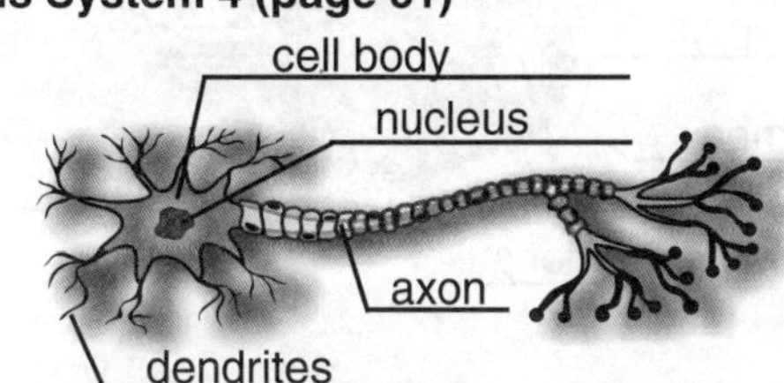

Nervous System 5 (page 31)
1. b   2. c   3. a   4. d

Nervous System 6 (page 32)
1. b   2. a   3. c

Nervous System 7 (page 32)
Sentences 1 and 3 should be checked.

Nervous System 8 (page 32)
"do" becomes "don't"
"dendrite" becomes "synapse"
"synapse" becomes "dendrite"
"fibers" becomes "chemicals"
"nucleus" becomes "axon"

Nervous System 9 (page 32)
1. T   2. F   3. T   4. T

Nervous System 10 (page 32)
1. cerebrum
2. cerebellum
3. brain stem

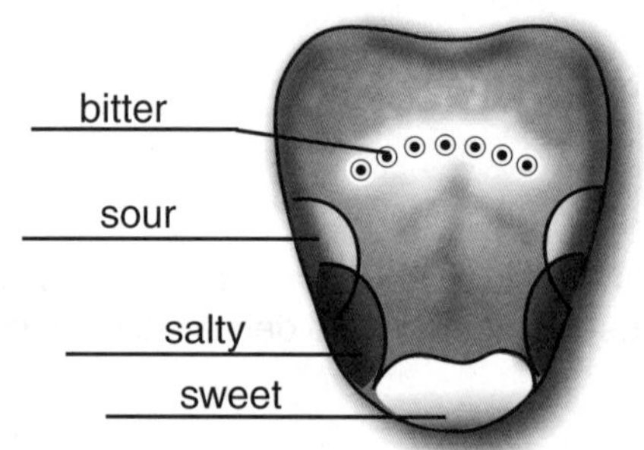

Nervous System 11 (page 33)
1. eyes   2. skin   3. ears   4. nose
5. tongue   6. tongue   7. ears   8. nose
9. eyes   10. skin

Nervous System 12 (page 33)
1. brain stem   2. cerebellum   3. cerebrum

Nervous System 13 (page 33)
1. cilia   2. mucus   3. nostrils

Nervous System 14 (page 33)
The following words should be circled: iris, pupil, cones, lens, rods, cornea, optic nerve, retina

Nervous System 15 (page 33)
Sentences 2 and 3 should be checked.

Nervous System 16 (page 34)

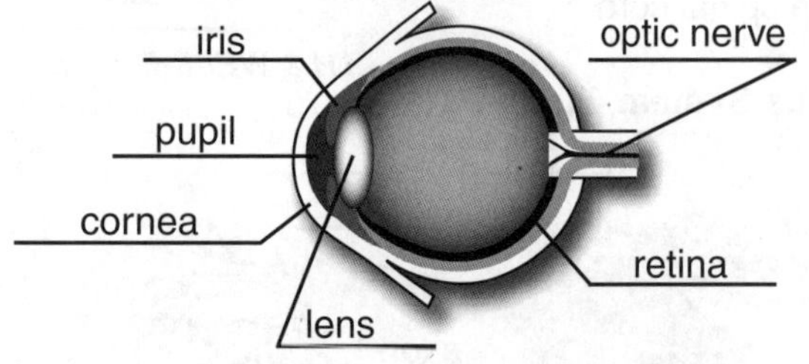

Nervous System 17 (page 34)
The skin

Nervous System 18 (page 34)
1. melanin   2. keratin
3. pores   4. hair follicles

Nervous System 19 (page 34)
a. 4   b. 3   c. 2   d. 1

Nervous System 20 (page 34)

Endocrine System 1 (page 35)
d. thyroid, e. hormone, b. thyroxine, a. metabolism, c. chemical

Endocrine System 2 (page 35)
1. F   2. T   3. T   4. F

Endocrine System 3 (page 35)
a. 3   b. 1   c. 4   d. 2

Endocrine System 4 (page 35)
1. pancreas   2. pituitary   3. thyroid

Endocrine System 5 (page 35)
1. c   2. e   3. b   4. a   5. d